Every Kid's Guide to
Overcoming Prejudice and Discrimination

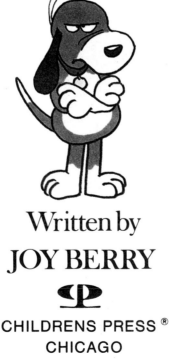

Written by

JOY BERRY

CHILDRENS PRESS ®
CHICAGO

About the Author and Publisher

Joy Berry's mission in life is to help families cope with everyday problems and to help children become competent, responsible, happy individuals. To achieve her goal, she has written over two hundred self-help books for children from birth through age twelve. Her work revolutionized children's publishing by providing families with practical, how-to, living skills information that was previously unavailable in children's books.

Joy gathered a dedicated team of experts, including psychologists, educators, child developmentalists, writers, editors, designers, and artists, to form her publishing company and to help produce her work.

The company, Living Skills Press, produces thoroughly researched books and audio-visual materials that successfully combine humor and education to teach subjects ranging from how to clean a bedroom to how to resolve problems and get along with other people.

Copyright © 1987 by Joy Berry
Living Skills Press, Sebastopol, CA
All rights reserved.
Printed in the United States of America

Managing Editor: Ellen Klarberg
Copy Editor: Kate Dickey
Contributing Editors: Libby Byers, Nancy Cochran, Maureen Dryden, Yona Flemming, Kathleen Mohr, Susan Motycka
Editorial Assistant: Sandy Passarino

Art Director: Laurie Westdahl
Design: Abigail Johnston, Laurie Westdahl
Production: Abigail Johnston
Illustrations designed by: Bartholomew
Inker: Linda Hanney
Colorer: Linda Hanney
Composition: Curt Chelin

You began having opinions when you were very young, and you will continue to have them for the rest of your life.

In **EVERY KID'S GUIDE TO OVERCOMING PREJUDICE AND DISCRIMINATION,** you will learn the following:

- what opinions are,
- where opinions come from,
- how to form opinions, and
- what prejudice and discrimination are.

An *opinion* is what a person thinks about something.

Whatever a person has an opinion about is called an *issue*.

If you agree with an issue, you have an opinion that is *for the issue.*

If you disagree with an issue, you have an opinion that is *against the issue.*

If you do not agree or disagree with an issue, your opinion is neither for nor against the issue. Your opinion is *neutral*.

If you have not decided whether you agree or disagree with an issue, your opinion is *undecided.*

It is important to know that no matter what your opinions are, they can change. You can alter what you think about an issue.

An opinion can become *stronger.* You can become *more* committed to what you think about an issue.

An opinion can become *weaker.* You can become *less* committed to what you think about an issue.

An opinion can become **different.** You can form a completely *new* opinion.

It is also important to understand that your opinions affect the way you behave.

Your reaction to people, places, or things is affected by what you think about them.

In the beginning of your life, your brain could form opinions. However, you did not have any opinions about anything.

You form your opinions as you live each day. Your surroundings affect the way you form opinions. The people and places that surround you and the experiences you have influence your thinking. These are called *environmental influences.*

The *people* in your life are environmental influences that affect the way you form opinions.

The people in your life include
- your family and relatives,
- your friends, and
- any other people with whom you come in contact.

The *places* in your life are environmental influences.

The places in your life include
- your home,
- your school,
- your church, synagogue, or temple
  (if you attend one),
- where you play, and
- where you work (if you work).

Your *experiences* are environmental influences.

The experiences in your life include
- what you see,
- what you read,
- what you hear,
- what you do, and
- what happens to you.

You can control much of the information you receive from environmental influences. But you *cannot* control it completely.

What you *can* control is how you respond to the information you receive.

You *can* control what kind of opinions you form from the information you receive.

Following these steps can help you form intelligent opinions:

Step 1. Pay attention to the information you receive from your environmental influences.

Step 2. Keep an open mind.

Remember there are at least two sides to every issue. The information you receive from one environmental influence is only one side of the issue. That one side might or might not be true.

Step 3. Gather information about the issue.

Talk about the issue with as many people as you can.
As you talk with them, consider these questions:

- What caused these people to think the way they think?
- Why do these people continue to think the way they think?

Read books, magazines, and newspapers that give you information about the issue.

Watch TV programs and listen to radio programs about the issue.

Continue to do research until you have all the information you need to form an intelligent opinion.

Step 4. Evaluate the information.

Consider each bit of information carefully. Try to
decide what information is true and what information
is false. Remember that people are not perfect and
that the information you receive from them might or
might not be true. This also applies to the information
you receive in books, newspapers, magazines, TV, and
radio.

Step 5. Form your opinion.

Decide whether you are

- for,
- against,
- neutral (neither for nor against), or
- undecided.

Step 6. Continue to evaluate your opinions.

Continue to keep an open mind. If you receive new information that proves your opinion is mistaken, change your opinion.

Do not feel bad about changing your opinion.
Changing an opinion that is mistaken can be a
positive thing to do.

If you form an opinion without following these six steps, you might *prejudge* an issue.

Prejudging means judging an issue before finding out all about it. A person who prejudges is often said to be prejudiced.

Because people's opinions affect the way they act, prejudice can lead to discrimination. Discrimination is treating another person unfairly because of a prejudice (a prejudged opinion).

There are many kinds of prejudice.

Physical prejudice is prejudging a person because of how the person looks.

Physical prejudice often causes discrimination.

Mental prejudice is prejudging a person because of

- how smart the person is,
- how much the person knows, or
- how well the person thinks.

Mental prejudice often causes discrimination.

Sexual prejudice is prejudging people because they are male or female.

Sexual prejudice often causes discrimination.

Age prejudice is prejudging people because of how
old they are.

Age prejudice often causes discrimination.

Racial prejudice is prejudging people because they are

- Caucasian,
- Asian, or
- Negroid.

Racial prejudice often causes discrimination.

National prejudice is prejudging people because of what area or what country they or their relatives come from.

National prejudice often causes discrimination.

Religious prejudice is prejudging a person because of the person's beliefs about God and religion.

Religious prejudice often causes discrimination.

Political prejudice is prejudging a person because of the kind of government and laws the person favors.

Political prejudice often causes discrimination.

Social prejudice is prejudging a person because of what the person does, where the person lives, or what group of people the person spends most of his or her time with.

Social prejudice often causes discrimination.

Economic prejudice is prejudging a person because of how much money a person has or what he or she owns.

Economic prejudice often causes discrimination.

When you discriminate against people, you can cause them to be left out of groups and activities. You can hinder them from fulfilling their potential.

When you discriminate against people, you can deprive yourself of having relationships that could enhance and enrich your life.

Prejudice and discrimination can be cruel and unfair and can be harmful to every person involved. This is why you must form each one of your opinions very carefully.

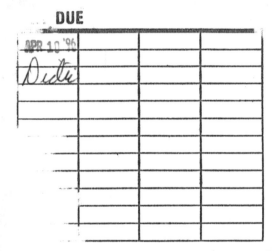